Trusting God When Bad Things Happen

Shelley Hitz

Trusting God When Bad Things Happen
© 2012 by Shelley Hitz

Published by Body and Soul Publishing
Printed In The United States of America

ISBN-13: 978-0615927015
ISBN-10: 0615927017

All scripture quotations, unless otherwise indicated, are taken from the Holy Bible, New International Version® 1973, 1978, 1984 by International Bible Society. Used by permission of Zondervan Publishing House. All rights reserved.

Scripture quotations marked NLT are taken from the Holy Bible, New Living Translation, copyright 1996, 2004. Used by permission of Tyndale House Publishers, Inc., Wheaton, Illinois 60189. All rights reserved.

Scripture quotations marked AMP are taken from the Amplified® Bible, Copyright © 1954, 1958, 1962, 1964, 1965, 1987 by The Lockman Foundation. Used by permission. (www.Lockman.org)

CONTENTS

PART ONE: IN THIS WORLD YOU WILL HAVE TROUBLE 1

BROKEN AND HURTING PEOPLE.. 2

IT ALL STARTED WITH A QUESTION FROM A HURTING GIRL............................ 4

PART TWO: BUT GOD...WHY?? 13

UNDERSTANDING GOD'S WAYS 14

THE WORLD IS MY CLASSROOM.. 15

THE POLAROID PICTURE... 17

LIFE IS A JOURNEY... 18

THE WORDS OF JOSEPH... 20

I'LL CLOSE WITH THIS POEM ENTITLED, ... 20

"THE WEAVER" 20

QUESTIONS FOR REFLECTION: 21

PART THREE: OUR VIEW OF GOD AND HOW IT IMPACTS US.......................... 23

OUR DIFFERENT VIEWS OF GOD... 24

A DISTORTED VIEW OF GOD 25

WHAT IS YOUR VIEW OF GOD?.. 27

DEVELOPING A HEALTHY VIEW OF GOD 28

BIBLICAL SAFEGUARDS FOR HEARING GOD'S VOICE.................................. 30

WHO DOES GOD SAY HE IS? 30

ACCORDING TO SCRIPTURE... 31

QUESTIONS FOR REFLECTION: 33

IN CLOSING... 37

APPENDIX: 39

EXCERPT FROM FORGIVENESS FORMULA 39

EXCERPT FROM UNSHACKLED AND FREE: TRUE STORIES OF FORGIVENESS 43

EXCERPT FROM FINDING HOPE IN THE MIDST OF TRAGEDY 49

Download Your FREE Book Extras

1.) Download 7 of Shelley's hand-drawn coloring pages for FREE.

2.) Download printable scripture cards.

3.) Watch powerful videos on the topic of Trusting God When Bad Things Happen and how Broken Crayons Still Color.

4.) Be encouraged by others' stories through the transcripts from the Broken Crayons Still Color podcast.

Get your FREE downloads here:
http://shelleyhitz.com/bookextras/

Part One:
In This World You Will Have Trouble

As a Christian, I have had a false expectation that life is supposed to be "perfect" and devoid of suffering. Therefore, when suffering came in my life, despite my faith and my prayers, I was devastated.

However, Jesus teaches us something much different. He says we are to expect trials, troubles and suffering. Jesus says in John 16:33, *In this world you will have trouble. But take heart! I have overcome the world!*

Notice that he doesn't say *you might* have trouble...he says *you will* have trouble. We are to expect difficult times to come realizing that we have the power of Jesus to help us overcome whatever may come our way.

Jesus also teaches in Matthew 5:44-45 that God sends both the sun and the rain to those who do good and those who do evil

> But I tell you: Love your enemies and pray for those who persecute you, that you may be sons of your Father in heaven. He causes the sun to rise on the evil and the good, and sends rain on the righteous and the unrighteous.

We are also encouraged to...

> ...consider it pure joy, my brothers, whenever you face trials of many kinds, because you know that the testing of your faith develops perseverance. Perseverance

1

must finish its work so that you may be mature and complete, not lacking anything....Blessed is the man who perseveres under trial because when he has stood the test, he will receive the crown of life God has promised to those who love Him.

James 1:2-4, 12

Again, notice that it doesn't say "*if you* face trials of many kinds"; it says "whenever you face trials of many kinds."

Broken and Hurting People

In the fall of 2007, I sensed God leading me to start a web site for teen girls. I had started speaking with my husband CJ and during breakout sessions, he would take the guys and cover the topic of pornography and I would take the girls and cover the topic of beauty. I would share with them my story of brokenness and the path I took to find my true beauty in Christ.

However, an hour just didn't seem like enough time. So, the website, www.FindYourTrueBeauty.com, was birthed. It became a way I could follow-up with the girls. It contains articles on body image, beauty, sex, dating, fashion, modesty, self-esteem and relationships. All from a biblical perspective.

As the site grew, I added articles on eating disorders, cutting and sexual abuse. I provide opportunities for girls to share their thoughts and opinions as well as their stories related to the topics on the site. I don't think anything could have prepared me for the deep pain that I would experience as I read their stories.

God began to open my eyes to the brokenness and pain that many carry with them every day. And for many of them, the way they were attempting to escape their emotional pain was through physical pain…either cutting themselves or through an eating disorder. Many of them had been sexually abused, verbally abused, physically abused or just neglected and ignored.

I was feeling overwhelmed with all the submissions coming in and the brokenness and despair I saw in these girls. As I was exercising at our local YMCA that night, I sensed God saying to me, *Shelley, I specialize in brokenness. Just like an orthopedic surgeon specializes in broken bones and torn muscles, I specialize in broken hearts. Bring them to me. I want to heal them.*

That night, I cried and grieved for all the hurting girls in this world. I felt a burden lifted from me as I surrendered their brokenness and pain to Him, *who heals the brokenhearted.* It's still hard to hear their stories, but God has helped me gain perspective. I began to realize that it is not my responsibility to "fix" them, but to pray for them and bring them to the One who can heal them, the One who specializes in healing broken hearts.

My eyes have been opened to the vast number of people suffering from pain and brokenness. And it is from that perspective that I sensed God asking me to write on the subject of "When Bad Things Happen" in this book. I have to be honest that I didn't want to write about this topic.

It is easy to be misunderstood and for people to debate the theology on why bad things happen. But, I feel I need to obey

God...and point you to Jesus, the One who specializes in brokenness. Ultimately, it will be in Jesus that true healing, freedom and life is found. I encourage you to come to Him with your questions and with your pain. More than anything, He wants to give you life and life to the fullest. Even when life doesn't seem to make sense.

It All Started With a Question From a Hurting Girl

When I think about the topic of "Why Bad Things Happen," my dialogue with Debby instantly comes to mind. I feel led to share our conversation with you because I believe there are others who have similar questions. I don't pretend to have all the answers, but I know Someone who does. And if you are struggling with this topic, I encourage you to continue your dialogue with God through prayer, journaling and searching His Word.

Debby had been sexually abused in her past and had many questions. Like many of us do. It's okay to ask questions and search for the truth. Unfortunately, many of us just keep our questions to ourselves. However, Debby was brave enough to verbalize the thoughts and the questions going around in her mind.

Here are Debby's initial questions

> With every GOOD there is EVIL or with every GOD there is a DEVIL. I was good and my devil was my abuser, why would a man so great allow such evil? He created man and woman, He was the first thing ever so

why create a devil? Why allow such sick people or spirits to exist?

Maybe I lack education or understanding of this but surely I should question this. Why should a person love such a powerful and creating God if He stepped back one day and allowed children to be hurt?

And Here is My Reply:

That's a very valid question and not an easy one to answer. I won't just try to give you a pat answer or try to explain away your hurt. Someone did something to you that was wrong.

And it hurt.

I believe God grieves when we hurt. So, why does He allow it? I don't think I'll fully know the answer to that question until I reach heaven.

But, in the meantime, one thing I do know is that the Bible says all evil originates from sin, and that all sin is caused by satan.

So, if satan causes all sin, who should we blame when evil things like this happen to us? God or satan? We should be blaming satan and not God.

Why does God allow it? Like I said, I have wrestled with this question. Between the sexual abuse that happened to me and my Grandma's murder, believe me, I have wrestled with this question.

Here is one thing to consider. God decided that He would give us free will. The ability to choose. I believe He did this because He wants to have a relationship with us where we choose to love Him...so we're not just robots in service to Him.

However, with free will comes the ability to choose to do good or evil. And the evil we see around the world is because people choose not to love God and obey Him.

If He forced us to obey Him, then He would be taking away free will and also taking away our ability to choose to love Him and have that kind of relationship with Him.

For instance, would you rather have someone say they love you because they choose to or because you are forcing them to say it? I think we all want to know someone is choosing us over everyone else in the world to love. Not just because they have to.

In John 10:10 the Bible tells us what Satan's mission statement is for our lives, *The thief (satan) comes only to steal and kill and destroy; I (Jesus) have come that they may have life, and have it to the full.*

Therefore, I believe anything that has stolen something from me (my innocence), killed my joy or destroyed something precious within me...is the work of satan and not God.

Debby had more questions...

I love the fact that you're replying to me and helping me no matter what I question, let me just take a moment to say thank you very much for this, I very much so appreciate it.

God is the creator or so I understand, why create satan in the first place? I mean no harm or offense with the questions I pose, I guess I'm like everyone, we all strive for answers to things that are not easily answered and I suppose that having faith is not something you can easily pick up and put down. I like things set in stone and if not I like to debate them to find a theory that is logical."

Here is My Reply:

I'm glad to listen and discuss, so I'm glad that you are here and asking your questions!!

I pray that you continue to get a little more clarity each day. Sometimes I say that something seems "clear as mud." Have you ever seen a glass of muddy water that you can't even see through, become clear after the glass sits awhile and the mud settles to the bottom? That's the picture I get for you. Right now everything is stirred up and confusing to understand, but over time and seeking God, the "mud" will settle and give you a clearer picture.

I want to answer your question about satan. You asked, "God is the creator or so I understand, so why create satan in the first place?" That is a good question and

7

makes sense to ask. Actually, the Bible says that satan was created originally as an angel and was created "blameless." However, like I mentioned before, God gives us free will to choose to love Him. This was the same for the angels.

God gave satan the choice of whether he wanted to choose God or choose evil. And he ended up choosing evil and was banished from heaven.

Ezekiel 28:12-19 describes what happened to satan, referring to him as the King of Tyre. *Son of man, take up a lament concerning the king of Tyre and say to him: This is what the Sovereign LORD says:*

'You were the model of perfection, full of wisdom and perfect in beauty.

'You were in Eden, the garden of God; every precious stone adorned you: ruby, topaz and emerald, chrysolite, onyx and jasper, sapphire, turquoise and beryl. Your settings and mountings were made of gold; on the day you were created they were prepared. You were anointed as a guardian cherub, for so I ordained you. You were on the holy mount of God; you walked among the fiery stones. You were blameless in your ways from the day you were created till wickedness was found in you. Through your widespread trade you were filled with violence, and you sinned. So I drove you in disgrace from the mount of God, and I expelled you, O guardian cherub, from among the fiery stones.

'Your heart became proud on account of your beauty, and you corrupted your wisdom because of your splendor. <u>So I threw you to the earth</u>; I made a spectacle of you before kings. By your many sins and dishonest trade you have desecrated your sanctuaries.

'So I made a fire come out from you, and it consumed you, and I reduced you to ashes on the ground in the sight of all who were watching. All the nations who knew you are appalled at you; you have come to a horrible end and will be no more.'"

Revelation 12:1-9 (emphasis mine) also describes what happened to satan. Satan is the dragon and the Son is Jesus. It talks about a "war in heaven" and how satan and his angels lost their place in heaven and were "hurled to the earth" where he now leads the "whole world astray."

> A great and wondrous sign appeared in heaven: a woman clothed with the sun, with the moon under her feet and a crown of twelve stars on her head. She was pregnant and cried out in pain as she was about to give birth. Then another sign appeared in heaven: an enormous red dragon with seven heads and ten horns and seven crowns on his heads. His tail swept a third of the stars out of the sky and flung them to the earth. The dragon stood in front of the woman who was about to give birth, so that he might devour her child the moment it was born. She gave birth to a son, a male child, who will rule all the nations with an iron scepter. And

her child was snatched up to God and to his throne. The woman fled into the desert to a place prepared for her by God, where she might be taken care of for 1,260 days. And there was war in heaven.

Michael and his angels fought against the dragon, and the dragon and his angels fought back. But he was not strong enough, and they lost their place in heaven. **The great dragon was hurled down - that ancient serpent called the devil, or satan, who leads the whole world astray. He was hurled to the earth, and his angels with him.**

Therefore, God created satan to be good and blameless...not evil. It was by satan's own choice to do evil and therefore be cast out of heaven. He is now at war and Revelations 12:12b says, *He is filled with fury, because he knows that his time is short.*

Therefore, I believe he does everything he can in the time he has before Jesus returns to "kill, steal and destroy." Does that make sense to you? Let me know if you still have questions about this.

Here is Debby's Response:

Okay that makes very good sense, it would be the same for every person, they choose a life of good or bad, and satan as well as others choose the wrong the way to live.

10

This is good I like it, however, does God not commit sin the second he throws satan to earth and burn him? Satan may be evil but killing him isn't really a good way to deal with him.

Here is My Answer:

Basically, satan was trying to take God's place and become God himself. He was trying to take over. And ultimately there is only room for one God.

God didn't kill him, but satan did lose his position in heaven. The Bible says that about one-third of the angels went with satan...and he started his own "kingdom" so to speak here on earth in the spiritual realm. Now he has demons that are under him and help him.

But, ultimately, satan's kingdom will not last forever. Only God's will.

I didn't hear from Debby again, but I trust that God planted seeds in her heart through His Word that will bear fruit. I still sometimes think of Debby and pray for her...and all the others that have questions similar to hers.

And I bring them to Jesus.

Part Two:
But God...Why??

When bad things happen in your life, have you ever asked God the simple one word question: "Why?"

I'll be honest. There is no easy answer for these types of questions. However, God is patient with us and willing to walk with us through our difficult questions.

I want you to know from the start that I'm not going to give you "pat answers." And I'm not going to pretend that I have it all figured out either. Because I don't.

But, I'm not going to let that stop me from sharing what I have learned. If this topic of *"Why Bad Things Happen"* is something you're struggling with, then I encourage you to continue to seek God and ask Him for His wisdom. He wants to give it to you.

Then you will call upon me and come and pray to me, and I will listen to you. You will seek me and find me when you seek me with all your heart. Jeremiah 29:12-13

If any of you lacks wisdom, he should ask God, who gives generously to all without finding fault, *and it will be given to him. But when he asks, he must* believe and not doubt, *because he who doubts is like a wave of the sea, blown and tossed by the wind. That man should not think he will receive anything from the Lord; he is a double-minded man, unstable in all he does.* James 1:5-8

Understanding God's Ways

I am convinced there are certain questions I won't know the answers to until I reach heaven.

It's like expecting my two year old niece to fully understand Calculus and Physics right now. She's not ready for it yet. It's just not going to make sense to her until her brain fully develops. And even then, these are still difficult subjects to fully grasp.

In a similar way, I realize that in my finite brain (my "two year old brain") there are certain things that just won't make sense to me on this earth. I just don't have the capacity in this human "equipment" to understand *everything* right now.

I Corinthians 13:12 says, *Now we see but a poor reflection as in a mirror; then we shall see face to face. Now I know in part; then I shall know fully, even as I am fully known.*

Those verses are talking about earth versus heaven. Right now I know in part, in heaven I shall know fully.

It's like having one piece of a puzzle and being able to say with certainty what picture the entire puzzle will create. You might have guesses, but you can't say with certainty what picture the puzzle piece creates, can you?

I've come to trust God with all the missing puzzle pieces in my life. I've come to trust that He has my best interests in mind and He will use the hard and difficult things in my life for good. You may not be at that same place today and that's okay. It took me time to get here. And a lot of wrestling with a lot of difficult questions.

Questions like:

> - God, why did you allow my Grandma to be murdered and my Grandpa to die a wrongful death?
> - God, why did my two cousins, Christa and Adam, die in car accidents as teenagers?
> - God, why did you allow sexual abuse to happen to me?
> - God, why didn't you restore my parents' marriage?

And I've come to a place of trust. Realizing that God's ways are higher than mine.

I'm the two year old with just a few pieces of the puzzle. God not only has all my "missing pieces," but he also has the "puzzle box top" and sees the entire picture.

> For my thoughts are not your thoughts, neither are your ways my ways, declares the Lord.
>
> As the heavens are higher than the earth, so are my ways higher than your ways and my thoughts than your thoughts. Isaiah 55:8-9 (NIV)

The World is My Classroom

The world is my classroom...The school of life offers some difficult courses, but it is in the difficult class that one learns the most–especially when the teacher is the Lord Jesus Himself. [13] Corrie ten Boom

I have to admit that at the age of thirty-four, I've already taken some pretty difficult courses in life. The school of life has not always been easy for me. And one of the most difficult "courses" I took was dealing with my parents' separation and divorce.

I prayed and prayed that God would restore my parents' marriage and bring my family back together. I had faith that He would do it. And yet, I didn't get the answer I'd hoped for.

And in the years that followed, it felt like an earthquake had come, destroying the foundation of my life. It hurt. It was painful. I didn't understand why God was allowing my family to be destroyed.

And yet I can see how, through this "earthquake" in my life, God has removed the rubble and has begun rebuilding, restoring and renewing something in me that I don't think could have happened any other way (Isaiah 61:4). He has used this difficult time in my life as a "refiner's fire" to purify me by bringing my impurities to the surface and removing them with His grace.

I now realize that instead of building the foundation of my life upon Jesus Christ, I had built the foundation of my life upon my family. And when my family crumbled, so did I.

It wasn't pretty. And it's a place I never want to go back to. Not even to visit.

I realize that, as Corrie ten Boom said, ...*it is in the difficult class that one learns the most.*[2] God was teaching me to rebuild my life with Him as my foundation and nothing else. He was teaching me to gain my satisfaction through Him and nothing else. He was stripping me of all my vices and addictions and helping me find true freedom.

It was hard for me…just ask my close friends and family.

The Polaroid Picture

Kay Warren[3] gives an illustration about a Polaroid picture that makes sense to me. Do you remember Polaroid cameras? These cameras take a picture and instantly produce a print copy. However, it takes time for the picture to develop and at first the picture looks fuzzy.

In the same way, Kay says certain circumstances in our lives will look fuzzy and unclear at first…it won't be until later that we will see the full picture.

When I was in the middle of my parents' separation that led to their divorce, the picture was fuzzy and unclear. I couldn't understand. It didn't make sense. Now I can see the good that God has brought out of this difficult situation in my life. Although I still don't have all the answers, the fuzzy picture is starting to become clear.

I can guarantee you that I would not be writing this book if I had not gone through that dark time. Instead, I was on a path to advance my Physical Therapy career. I was all about me. And I was very self-centered.

But, this is what the past is for! Every experience God gives us, every person He puts in our lives is the perfect preparation for the future that only He can see.[4] Corrie ten Boom

I can see now that God was preparing me for the future and the ministry He had for me.

Athletes know and expect their training to be hard and rigorous. They endure suffering because they are looking ahead to the game or the race.

Do you not know that in a race all the runners run, but only one gets the prize? Run in such a way as to get the prize. <u>Everyone who competes in the games goes into strict training.</u> They do it to get a crown that will not last; but we do it to get a crown that will last forever. I Corinthians 9:24-25

Not only that, I can now see that God is using the difficult times I have gone through and my story of healing to help others.

*Praise be to the God and Father of our Lord Jesus Christ, the Father of compassion and the God of all comfort, who comforts us in all our troubles, **so that we can comfort those in any trouble with the comfort we ourselves have received from God.** For just as the sufferings of Christ flow over into our lives, so also through Christ our comfort overflows.* 2 Corinthians 1:3-5 (emphasis mine)

Life is a Journey...

I wanted to share a poem I wrote for my dad and step-mom when my dad re-married in May of 2008.

Even though I didn't like the details of the journey or agree with or approve of decisions that were made, I could finally see the "gift" that this journey gave me. God used it to bring healing in my life that I don't think could have come any other way. Here is the poem.

You have both been on a journey that led to today. Your paths have intersected and life will never be the same. As your journey has unfolded these past few years, it has greatly impacted mine.

To be honest, I walked through many dark and painful days as life seemed to unravel before me. It seemed like everything I once knew came crashing down. Nothing was the same and I didn't like it. I grieved deeply and many tears were shed.

But, through the pain, a miracle happened. A rescue. I was led down the path of forgiveness and then, slowly, healing began to take place within me. A new freedom and joy. A depth of grace and love I had never known before.

Jesus rescued me and brought healing to my pain. I am a different person now.

And even though these have been some of the hardest years of my life, I am so grateful for the gift this journey, your journey, has given me. I would not be who I am today if it wasn't for you.

So, today, I wish the same blessing for each of you. Grace, forgiveness, healing, freedom, wholeness. Rescue. That the fingerprints of Jesus would be seen upon your lives and evident to everyone around you. That Jesus would be at the center of your heart and your home.

Matthew 6:33 says, "But seek first his kingdom and his righteousness, and all these things will be given to you as well."

Love,
Shelley

The Words of Joseph...

I encourage you to go back and read the story of Joseph in Genesis. It is a powerful story of God using the difficult times in Joseph's life for good. His brothers sold him into slavery. He ended up in Egypt and through a course of circumstances, ended up in charge of a project that would literally save those in Egypt and the surrounding countries, including Joseph's family, from starvation.

Joseph told his brothers who sold him into slavery, *You intended to harm me, but God intended it for good to accomplish what is now being done, the saving of many lives.* Genesis 50:20

I can now see how God is using the painful experiences in my past for good. The enemy meant to harm and destroy me, but God has used it for good. And He wants to do the same in your life.

I'll close with this poem entitled, "The Weaver"

My life is but a weaving, between my God and me,
I do not choose the colors, He worketh steadily,
Oftimes He weaveth sorrow, and I in foolish pride,

Forget He sees the upper, and I the underside.
Not till the loom is silent, and shuttles cease to fly,
Will God unroll the canvas and explain the reason why.
The dark threads are as needful in the skillful Weaver's hand,
As the threads of gold and silver in the pattern He has
planned.
--ANONYMOUS

Questions for Reflection:

1. I encourage you to stop right now and pray. Ask God to help you as you tackle this difficult topic of "why bad things happen." He will empower you and help you face even the most difficult questions and the deepest pain. You might want to pray a prayer of surrender. If so, you can pray something like this,

Lord, I surrender to you my heart, mind and will and ask that you lead me through this time of journaling and prayer. Help me as I bring my questions, pain and brokenness to you. I acknowledge your power to grant me wisdom (James 1:5) and ask that You come right now and help me do what I cannot do myself. Amen.

2. In your journal, list some difficult or painful experiences from your life. Then, write out any questions you've had on this topic of "why bad things happen." Are there things in your life that you are struggling to understand?

3. Go back through this chapter and find any illustrations or scriptures that stood out to you. How do you think this relates to your questions? Are there any

additional insights God is giving you or any additional scriptures?

4. You may want to take your journal and your questions to a counselor, pastor or close friend to discuss and pray over.

5. Here is a recommended closing prayer. *Lord, I realize that I may never have all the answers to my questions this side of heaven. But, I ask that you continue to reveal Yourself to me, giving me wisdom and understanding. Help me to trust You with the things I still don't understand.*

I thank You that You have promised to walk through every painful trial with me. That You will never leave me or forsake me. I thank You that even when other people fail me, You will never fail me. Help me to put my trust in You and not in people or circumstances. I thank You that even if I can't see it, you promise to bring good out of the pain in my life (Romans 8:28). I love you, I worship you, I trust you. Amen.

Part Three:
Our View of God and How it Impacts Us

When a train goes through a tunnel and it gets dark, you don't throw away the ticket and jump off. You sit still and trust the engineer. --Corrie ten Boom

When life gets dark through the various "tunnels" we face, it may be difficult to "trust the engineer." In this analogy, our engineer is God and our tunnels are the painful situations that come into our lives. We will all experience them to one degree or another. They may come as a season of darkness where we have difficulty hearing God's voice or seeing His hand in our lives. And at that time, we may want to "throw away our ticket and jump off the train." Or give up and "throw in the towel," so to speak.

And at those times, when hurtful events come into our lives and we can't see past the pain, our view of God can become distorted.

Somehow we never see God in failure, but only in success and happiness – a strange attitude for people who have the cross at the center of their faith. --Cheryl Forbes

Gwen Ebner says, *The way we view God and ourselves is a fundamental issue of life because all things flow from our belief about God and ourselves. These viewpoints affect everything about us–our responses, reactions, what we believe, what we say, how we act and react, how we relate to family and friends, how we parent, and how we minister.* [5]

Think about it. When you view someone as loving and trustworthy, you will be more open to their thoughts and advice. However, if someone has hurt you, lied to you or cheated you in the past, you are less likely to listen to them.

Our Different Views of God

Our view of God is usually formed early in life from various influences including our parents, family members, church, friends, media, school teachers etc.

There was an interesting study conducted by Baylor University that contained twenty-nine questions about God's character and behavior.[6] There were two specific dimensions of God this study focused on: 1. how involved or engaged God is in our daily lives and 2. how angry God is towards our sins (punishing, severe and wrathful).

From the findings, the researchers came up with five different views of God. There is a graphic of this that you can see outlined at this link: http://www.bodyandsoulpublishing.com/four-views-of-god/

Here are the five views of God from this study:

1. **The Benevolent God** (23% overall): Highly involved in our lives, but less angry and more forgiving of our sins.
2. **The Authoritarian God** (31.4% overall): Highly involved in our lives, but also highly angry at our sins and punishing.
3. **The Distant God** (24.4% overall): Distant and uninvolved in our lives, but not especially angry either.
4. **The Critical God** (16% overall): Distant and uninvolved in our lives as well as highly angry at our sins and punishing.

5. **Atheist** (5.2% overall): God does not exist.

The researchers found that our view of God tends to impact our actions. For instance, those who viewed God as distant and uninvolved in their daily lives were less likely to pray several times a day (Critical God 6.5% and Distant God 7% vs. Authoritarian God 54.8% and Benevolent God 31.7%).[7]

The researchers also found that a person's view of God tends to have an impact on beliefs about sex and marital issues. For example, the percentage of people who believe pre-marital sex is always wrong is as follows: Authoritarian God 58.7%, Benevolent God 35.9%, Critical God 18.8% and Distant God 7.5%.[8]

They found similar findings for beliefs on co-habitation, pornography, abortion and homosexuality. Therefore, we can see how our view of God has the potential to deeply impact our lives and the decisions we make every day.

A Distorted View of God

Sometimes, our view of God can be influenced by hurtful situations that come into our lives.

Looking back, I can see that I adopted a distorted view of God due to several painful experiences in my past, including my Grandma's murder. I saw God as distant and uncaring. I felt like He wasn't there for me during these difficult situations. I felt like He let me down and disappointed me. Therefore, how could I fully trust Him with my entire life? How could I trust Him to make the best decisions for my life? Therefore, I concluded I couldn't fully trust God and decided to trust in myself instead. This distorted view of God held me back from growing in my faith and maturing.

Instead, I developed a humanistic, or self-centered, view of life that led to self-effort and workaholism. I stayed active in the church, but kept God at a distance partly due to my distorted view of Him. I can relate to Mackenzie, the main character in the book *The Shack*, who struggled to trust God after a traumatic event occurred in his life.

> God says to him, *"You try to make sense of the world in which you live based on a very small and incomplete picture of reality. It is like looking at a parade through the tiny knothole of hurt, pain, self-centeredness, and power, and believing you are on your own and insignificant. All of these contain powerful lies. You see pain and death as ultimate evils and God as the ultimate betrayer, or perhaps, at best, as fundamentally untrustworthy....*
>
> *"The real underlying flaw in your life, Mackenzie, is that you don't think that I am good. If you knew I was good and that everything – the means, the ends, and all the processes of individual lives – is all covered by my goodness, then while you might not always understand what I am doing, you would trust me. But you don't...*
>
> *"Trust is the fruit of a relationship in which you know you are loved. Because you do not know that I love you, you cannot trust me."* [9]

What is Your View of God?

Some of us may have a very *legalistic* or *rules-based* view of God. In this instance, He tends to be seen as a harsh judge that is angered when we don't perform perfectly. Therefore, we see God as unapproachable and our relationship is based primarily on fear and rules.

Others may see God as *permissive* and too kind to punish us. He is lenient, noncommittal, passive, and easy going. This tends to be a relativistic perspective that many in our culture adopt today. In this view of God we don't have a close relationship and rarely approach God. Instead of being afraid of God, we have disrespect for God.

Finally, a more *accurate* view of God is one where we see God as open, generous, balanced, collaborative, honest, dependable and responsible. We find God approachable, are comfortable in his presence and interact with Him out of a relationship of grace. We have a healthy fear and respect of God and realize that He judges justly.

Stop and take a moment to consider how God's voice sounds to you. This may help you better understand your view of God.

To You, is God's Voice...
Harsh or Loving?
Condemning or Grace-based?
Angry or Caring?
Critical or Accepting?
Demeaning or Affirming?
Hurtful or Kind?

Far off or Close by?
Silent or Present?
Demanding or Fair?
Perfectionistic or Forgiving?

I believe it is important to have a healthy view of God *before* a crisis happens. Otherwise, we'll view God through the crisis instead of viewing the crisis through God and His character.

Developing a Healthy View of God

If our view of God has been skewed through painful experiences, through being injured by an authority figure, or by having experienced spiritual abuse sometime in our life, we will need to address those wounds in order for us to feel safe moving close to God. A good Godly counselor or spiritual director can be a great resource in dealing with the obstacles that have closed down our heart to God. [10] -- Gwen Ebner

One of the best ways to develop a healthy view of God is getting to know Him through the scriptures. However, it is one thing to know who God is through the scriptures *intellectually* through reading and studying the Bible. Knowing about God and knowing Him personally are two different things. Therefore, is important to have more than just an intellectual understanding of God. Our knowledge of Him must travel the distance from our heads to our hearts. Heart knowledge of God will only come through personally experiencing His characteristics by spending time with Him and opening our heart to Him through a personal relationship.

One way that I've been able to open my heart to God and experience Him in a deeper way is through a form of prayer I call "two-way journaling." Not only am I talking to God by journaling my thoughts and feelings, but I am listening to Him as well by journaling what I sense Him saying to me in my heart.

Mark Virkler[11] gives four keys to hearing God's voice as follows:

> 1. **Stillness**: Quieting ourselves down. *"Be still and know that I am God."* Psalm 46:10
>
> 2. **Vision**: Fixing our eyes on Jesus. *Let us fix our eyes on Jesus, the author and perfecter of our faith.* Hebrews 12:2
>
> 3. **Spontaneity**: Realize that God's voice often comes as spontaneous thoughts within our minds. *If anyone is thirsty, let him come to me and drink. Whoever believes in me, as the Scripture has said, **streams of living water will flow from within him.*** *By this he meant the Spirit, whom those who believed in Him were later to receive.* John 7:37-39 (emphasis mine)
>
> 4. **Journaling**: Write out your prayers as a conversation, two-way journaling. Then the Lord said, *'Write down the revelation...'* Habakkuk 2:2

As I have learned to recognize God's voice and sense what He is saying to me through the Holy Spirit, I have grown leaps and bounds in my relationship with Him. I encourage you to do the same. However, I give you a note of caution. This is not for anyone and everyone. Before you begin two-way journaling, you should incorporate a few Biblical safeguards for hearing God's voice as follows.

Biblical Safeguards for Hearing God's Voice

1. You are a Christ follower, having accepted Jesus as your Savior and have had your sins cleansed by His blood.

2. You accept the Bible as the inerrant Word of God. All your journaling should line up with the truths in the Bible.

3. You show your love and respect for God by your commitment to knowing His Word and obeying what He shows you. Even if you are a new believer, you can read through the entire New Testament in a couple days.

4. You have two or three spiritual advisors to whom you share your journaling and ask for their input on a regular basis. *In the multitude of counselors there is safety.* Proverbs 11:14

Who Does God Say He Is?

We all probably have a slightly different view of God due to the different influences in our lives. However, who does God truly say He is according to His Word, the Bible?

According to Scripture

God Is Changeless. *"I the LORD do not change. So you, O descendants of Jacob, are not destroyed"* Malachi 3:6

Whatever is good and perfect comes to us from God above, who created all heaven's lights. Unlike them, He never changes or casts shifting shadows James 1:17

God Is All Powerful. *O Sovereign Lord! You have made the heavens and earth by Your great power. Nothing is too hard for You!* Jeremiah 32:17

God Is All Knowing. *Oh, what a wonderful God we have! How great are His riches and wisdom and knowledge! How impossible it is for us to understand His decisions and His methods! For who can know what the Lord is thinking? Who knows enough to be His counselor?* Romans 11:33, 34

God Is Everywhere. *Where can I go from Your Spirit? Where can I flee from Your presence? If I go up to the heavens, You are there; if I make my bed in the depths, You are there. If I rise on the wings of the dawn, if I settle on the far side of the sea, even there Your hand will guide me, Your right hand will hold me fast.* Psalm 139:7–10

God Is Eternal. *I am the Alpha and the Omega, says the Lord God, who is, and who was, and who is to come, the Almighty.* Revelation 1:8

God Is Holy. *Who else among the gods is like You, O Lord? Who is glorious in holiness like You-so awesome in splendor, performing such wonders?* Exodus 15:11

Holy, holy, holy is the LORD Almighty; the whole earth is full of his glory. Isaiah 6:3

God Is Love. *May your roots go down deep into the soil of God's marvelous love. And may you have the power to understand, as all God's people should, how wide, how long, how high, and how deep His love really is* Ephesians 3:17, 18

God Is Truth. *God is not a man, that He should lie. He is not a human, that He should change His mind. Has He ever spoken and failed to act? Has He ever promised and not carried it through?* Numbers 23:19

Jesus said, *I am the way, the truth, and the life.* John 14:6

God Is Wisdom. *Oh, the depth of the riches of the wisdom and knowledge of God! How unsearchable his judgments, and his paths beyond tracing out!* Romans 11:33

God Is Just. *I, the Lord, search all hearts and examine secret motives. I give all people their due rewards, according to what their actions deserve.* Jeremiah 17:10

God is Compassionate. *The Lord is full of compassion and mercy.* James 5:11

The Lord comforts His people and will have compassion on His afflicted ones. Isaiah 49:13

God is Faithful. *O Lord God of hosts, who is a mighty one like unto You, O Lord? And Your faithfulness is round about You [an essential part of You at all times].* Psalm 89:88 (AMP)

Because of the LORD's great love we are not consumed, for his compassions never fail. They are new every morning; great is your faithfulness. Lamentations 3:22-23

If you've grown up with a distorted view of God, it may take you time to replace your current view of God with a healthy one. But, don't give up. Take one step at a time and continue spending time with the God of the universe. He loves you and longs to spend time with you!

> Everything about our lives—our attitudes, motives, desires, actions, and even our words—is influenced by our view of God. Whether our problems are financial, moral, or emotional, whether we are tempted by lust, worry, anger, or insecurity, our behavior reflects our beliefs about God. We can trace all our human problems to our view of God.[12] –Bill Bright

For more resources to help you develop a healthy view of God, go to www.DiscoverGod.com.

Questions for Reflection:

> 1. I encourage you to stop right now and pray. You might want to pray a prayer of surrender. If so, you can pray something like this,
>
> *Lord, I surrender to you my heart, mind and will and ask that you lead me through this time of journaling and prayer. Help me to be willing to deal with the issues of my past that are hindering my spiritual growth, including a distorted view of who You are. I*

acknowledge Your power to overcome any barriers in my heart that keep me from You. Amen.

2. Refer back to the chart on the different views of God (Benevolent, Authoritarian, Critical, Distant, Atheist). In your journal, write out the view of God that best describes your current belief. Then write out what influences in your life have most impacted this belief (parents, friends, media, school teachers, church, traumatic experiences, etc.).

3. In addition, would you say you've had a legalistic/rules based view of God, a permissive view of God or a more accurate view of God (open, generous, balanced, collaborative, honest, dependable and responsible)?

If you tend to have a legalistic/rules based view of God or a permissive view of God, I encourage you to pray and ask God to give you a more accurate view of Himself through His Word and a personal relationship with Him in your heart.

4. Circle the words below that apply to you.

To You, is God's Voice...
Harsh or Loving?
Condemning or Grace-based
Angry or Caring
Critical or Accepting
Demeaning or Affirming
Hurtful or Kind
Far off or Close by

Silent or Present
Demanding or Fair
Perfectionistic or Forgiving

5. I encourage you to begin your journey toward a healthy view of God (or continue it). This includes time reading His Word, the Bible and communicating with God through prayer. I encourage you to start by reading the story of Jesus' life in the gospels (Matthew, Mark, Luke and John). Even if you've read them before, ask the Holy Spirit to be your Teacher and show you what you need to know. Write down what you learn about God through his son Jesus in your journal and any questions that arise.

6. I also encourage you to begin two-way journaling only if you have met all the Biblical safeguards discussed above. You can begin with a simple question like, "Lord, what would you like to say to me today?" or "Lord, how do you see me?" It helps me to have soft instrumental music playing in the background and to visualize Jesus there with me.

7.   Here is a recommended closing prayer. *"Lord, I admit that at times I have a distorted view of You, whether from past experiences, family, friends or the media. I ask for forgiveness for the lies I have believed about who You are and forgive myself for believing those lies.*

'Bring healing to me in this area by replacing the lies I have believed with Your Truth so that I can have a healthy view of who You are. I realize that this impacts

me greatly, in almost every area of my life! Teach me through Your Word about your character and continue to draw me closer to Yourself through prayer. I open my heart to You and am willing to walk in faith in the areas I still don't completely understand. I love you, I worship you, I trust you. Amen."

In Closing...

Jesus never promised us that life would be easy. On the contrary, as followers of Jesus, we are promised persecution and suffering. However, He has promised to be with us every step of the way.

Download Your FREE Book Extras

1.) Download 7 of Shelley's hand-drawn coloring pages for FREE.

2.) Download printable scripture cards.

3.) Watch powerful videos on the topic of Trusting God When Bad Things Happen and how Broken Crayons Still Color.

4.) Be encouraged by others' stories through the transcripts from the Broken Crayons Still Color podcast.

Get your FREE downloads here:
http://shelleyhitz.com/bookextras/

Forgiveness Formula
Appendix:

Finding Lasting Freedom In Christ

"Trusting God When Bad Things Happen" is part of the award-winning and powerful book *"Forgiveness Formula: Finding Lasting Freedom in Christ."* Read the introduction to Forgiveness Formula below.

I (CJ) used to hate running with a passion. I just couldn't see the point unless I was running with a ball in my hands. I looked at this "sport" as a legal means of torture and punishment. I loathed that burning sensation in my lungs, the lactic acid build up in muscles throughout my body, and the exhaustion and fatigue I felt hours after crossing a finish line.

Wanna hear something wild? Now I absolutely LOVE running with a passion, go figure! You might even say I've become somewhat of a running addict. Do I still experience the burning sensation in my lungs? Yep. How about the lactic acid build up in my muscles? Affirmative. And the exhaustion and fatigue? They still show up at times as well.

So what's the difference you might ask? I've simply learned to embrace these "enemies" as things that will help me grow stronger as a runner and enable me to push harder than I did before.

Still, there are some days where it seems more difficult to stay motivated than others. February 12, 2009 was one such day. Once I finally got myself out the door, I soon realized this would be no easy eight-mile training run. Coming off a nasty chest cold didn't help either. Two words: wheezing and hacking. Look them up in Webster's and see what you come up with. Though the local weather man said it was thirty degrees outside, the wind chill factor made it feel like low twenties. During most of the run, this wind gusted up to forty mph, hitting me from the side and head-on with such ferocity it seemed as if all eleven guys on the Pittsburgh Steelers defense were lining up to take shots at me from all angles!

Not only was the wind a factor, but two miles in I began encountering some hills I wasn't expecting in the area of Michigan my wife Shelley and I were visiting. Strong wind combined with hills? This was too good to be true!

One thing that has helped me stay motivated on tough days like these is being signed up for upcoming races. I'm a person who enjoys setting race day goals and then putting in the training necessary in order to see those goals achieved. I knew the physical pain and agony my body was going through as I endured this day of wind resistance and hill training would be nice to have in the bank when it came time to race in less than a month.

And so it is in this journey we call Life. Part of being human in this world we inhabit means we endure pain, struggle, and resistance in the physical, mental, social, emotional and spiritual realms. How each person chooses to deal with that pain varies from one person to another. And though none of us would sign up to endure these "strong winds," if we're honest, we can look back on our lives and see that these things play a role in shaping us into who we are today (for better or for worse).

We have a myriad of answers, remedies and quick fixes that sometimes work to dull the pain in the short-term but never work over the long-term. Some of these things include chocolate, coffee, alcohol, drugs, sex, TV, pornography, video games, movies, shopping, recreation, self-injury and even suicide. And the list goes on...

The book you're now reading is written by two broken and fragile human beings who are far from perfect. We've attempted to numb our own pain with many of the things on that list above without any lasting success.

Neither are we experts who decided to write down information from our "vast stores of knowledge" with the purpose of making you, the reader, feel like a gnat.

We simply want to share some things that made ALL the difference regarding how we dealt with and continue to deal with pain and loss in our own lives. We hope you'll see us as two hungry beggars who found some bread and now want to point others to that bread. By the way, Jesus did say he's the Bread of Life.

Shelley and I believe every reader can benefit from what we share in these pages, whether you've endured varying levels of pain or struggle in your own life or you know someone who has. It's our prayer that God uses this book as a tool to bring healing, hope and a newfound freedom to people from all walks of life.

For those of you who consider yourselves to be followers of the teachings of Jesus, we hope and pray you're strengthened in your faith and challenged to live out those teachings in new ways. And for those of you who still have many unanswered questions about this Jesus, we encourage you to continue exploring at your own pace while reading the stories of two fellow travelers.

Maybe you've been searching for that formula that will help you make sense of your life. Come, join us as we explore the *Forgiveness Formula.*

Continue reading! Get your copy of "*Forgiveness Formula: Finding Lasting Freedom in Christ*" here:

http://www.amazon.com/dp/B0065USDB2

Available in both print and eBook versions.

Excerpt from Unshackled and Free: True Stories of Forgiveness

Forgiving an Unfaithful Spouse
Submitted by Janet Perez Eckles

He came home from work one evening and, with a cold and indifferent tone, not at all typical for him, my husband Gene frowned and cleared his throat. "Let's go for a ride, we need to talk."

His demeanor, somber and aloof puzzled me.

I threw on my bright red sweater and off-white corduroy pants. I don't know why, but details of the clothing I wear in moments of intense emotion are vividly engraved in the depths of my memory. I rushed to comb my hair and joined him as he silently walked me to the car. He opened the door, and I slipped into the passenger's seat. Clueless about what he wanted to talk about, I clicked on my seat belt. He started the engine and we rode silently as the car took us out of our neighborhood without any specific destination.

The Betrayal

"What's wrong?" I finally asked, my hand sweaty and my stomach tight.

He drew in a long breath and spat words that seared my soul, "I'm not happy …I've been wanting to tell you this for a long time." I held my breath, "There's another person in my life." His tone rang sad and at the same time indifferent, "She works with me and I've been confiding in her." The words that followed scorched my ears and stabbed rejection into my stomach.

"I don't feel well," I muttered. That cold black bucket seat suddenly felt like an electric chair, sending painful impulses of burning bolts through me. His feeble explanations and justifications eluded me. My concentration turned to visions of me and our three little boys added to the countless homes without fathers.

Trying to Survive

As weeks swept by, my house was no longer a home, but a pile of emotional rubble. My outward silence masked the turmoil that exploded inside me.

We made one more attempt. A secular counselor advised, "No sense in continuing a relationship that has been broken."

Alone and angry, I felt I was sinking deeper into the sand of sorrow. And though I'd grown up in church, I was stuck in spiritual infancy. I believed in God superficially, but deep down, I trusted in my own abilities. I'd felt satisfied with my life which, up to then, had followed a nearly perfect path. But now I desperately pounded through a dark alley, chased by shameful failure and rejection. With each step, I'd complain, and begged God for an answer. But His response of silence further intensified my anguish.

A Glimmer of Hope

Then, a dim light flickered through the fog when a friend invited me to her Christian church. And while sitting still,

Bible teachings reached my heart and caused me to listen, really listen. Eventually, my sobbing stopped, and a powerful verse flung my blindfold off:

"...seek first the kingdom of God... and all these things will be added to you."

~Matthew 6:33, ESV

I had been seeking my husband's love, his devotion, and the restoration of our marriage-that had been first in my list of priorities, not God. I swallowed hard in blatant awareness of my mistake, and I vowed to obey Him, no matter what.

Looking back, I had wondered about God's silence. But now, I realize He wasn't silent at all, it was my relentless ranting that drowned out His loving whisper. It was the forceful focus on my pain that blinded me from seeing the way out.

My New Path

And now, with a clear view of my new path, my anger and self-pity turned to constant prayer for my husband. Renewed security in God fluttered through my heart. And instead of tormenting thoughts, sleep came back at night as well as calmness during the day. Diligent application of Bible verses gave me renewed clarity and focus.

Though I blinked tears back, courage and confidence nudged me to address the issue once again. But this time, rather than a confrontation, I vowed it would be a peaceful dialogue.

"I didn't force you to marry me," I said with outward calmness. "And I won't force you to stay either," my heart

45

thumped. "Jesus will be the Father our sons might not have, and He will be the husband who'll never leave me."

An Unbelievable Turn of Events

Some days went by. Gene came home and asked to talk. He clasped my hand and held it tight, "I made a decision too." He said with conviction in his voice, "I will continue with our marriage. I'll be devoted to you and the kids."

Though my heart did a cartwheel, I held my words. Unlike before, my emotions wouldn't guide my reactions. Instead, God's wisdom would allow my response to glide with wisdom and poise. I accepted his decision, but caution still whispered way inside. I wasn't sure his words would turn to actions, but when he followed through I put another condition-that we needed to make a drastic change; we'd have to pray together.

He agreed.

The Most Difficult Hurdle

I heaved a deep sigh and braced myself to jump the most difficult hurdle-to forgive him. The choice was clear-nurse that wound, continue to look at it, dwell on it, and keep it fresh-or forgive, heal and watch it disappear. I chose the latter. And when I did, sweet freedom ushered in. The window of joy let in a fresh breeze of confidence. Gene wasn't married to that insecure young woman anymore. Forgiveness had dressed me with security, dignity and grace.

As we plan our next anniversary, celebrating 36 years of marriage, we dance to the melody of God's Word. Gene took the first step of repentance, and I followed with firm strides of forgiveness. And to my delight, we still follow the rhythm of God's symphony directing our renewed marriage fueled with revived romance.

Unshackled and Free: True Stories of Forgiveness contains stories from 33 different people that will encourage and inspire you. Get your copy to continue reading here:

http://www.amazon.com/dp/B007F1FQ4C

Available in print and eBook versions.

Excerpt from

Finding Hope in the Midst of Tragedy

I recently heard the word hope described as this acronym: Hold On, Pain Ends. And I have found that to be so true in my own life. One of my heroes of the faith and Nazi prison camp survivor, Corrie ten Boom, describes it this way, "When a train goes through a tunnel and it gets dark, you don't throw away the ticket and jump off. You sit still and trust the engineer."

This book is my own personal journey to finding hope after a tragedy hit our family. However, I did not want this book to be my story alone. Instead, I wanted it to be a resource for you to find hope in the midst of your own difficulties. That is why I have added the sections that you will see through the book called, "From My Life to Yours," where I add journaling prompts and suggested prayers for you to apply what you are learning to your life. I pray that God leads you to find His hope no matter what you are walking through.

My Story

I had no clue how drastically my life would change this year. I thought some of my worst days were over. I thought that I had dealt with enough trials for one lifetime. However, on July 1st 2009, that all changed when my dad, Chuck Sandstrom, was assaulted. Once again, a violent act was committed against our family and this time it hit even closer to home, my dad. Dad was assaulted so severely that it left him in a coma for almost six weeks and resulted in a severe Traumatic Brain Injury (TBI).

At first I was in shock and was numb. But, eventually, many emotions began to surface. Anger, grief, pain, unforgiveness. I heard myself saying, "Lord, it's not fair. Why our family, AGAIN? I don't know if I can handle this." I realized it was time for me to walk through the path of forgiveness once again and choose to trust God with the pain, the hurt and the unknowns of this tragedy. And He led me down a path to find hope...hope in the midst of tragedy.

I won't lie to you. It hasn't been an easy road. And it's not over. Dad is now out of the coma and progressing every day. He is walking, talking and eating again. He is now home. But, there is a long road ahead. Dad still needs a lot of speech therapy and cognitive therapy. He may end up losing his job. And they still haven't found his perpetrator. Yes, there is still a long road ahead of us. But, looking back, I can see God's Presence with us every step of the way. Every tear, every emotion, every joy, every disappointment. He has been here.

I've found out once again that what Jesus teaches is applicable to real-life. In the midst of pain, tragedy and some of the most difficult days of my life, Jesus brought me hope.
And He wants to do the same for you, if you'll seek Him and apply His teachings to your life.

What I share in this book in my "journal" that I posted on my blog through the difficult days after my dad's assault, coma and resulting traumatic brain injury. I opened my heart for all to see my journey…my journey to finding hope in the midst of tragedy. I pray God uses this book to encourage and inspire you.

July 1, 2009: About My Dad's Assault

On July 1st, 2009 my dad was assaulted and suffered a severe traumatic brain injury (TBI) that left him in a coma for weeks. We didn't know if he would survive that first day and then the doctors told us that he might never wake up. However, we have seen God work miracles in the midst of this tragedy.

The Media…

The first article printed in the media about Dad was in the Barberton Herald. Several other stories were published later in the Akron Beacon Journal, Channel 5 News and the Findlay Courier. However, as usually happens with news stories, all the details were not 100% accurate.

Here are a couple items to clear up…

There was a vehicle parked at my dad's rental property that was not registered to his tenants. It had been there for weeks and he decided to call the police and have it towed.

My dad's assailant, Michael, was not a tenant but a relative of a tenant. And witnesses say my dad was not in an argument. According to neighbors, Dad was attempting to reason with a highly volatile person about the towing of this unregistered vehicle that had been on the premises for weeks. Basically, he was a landlord taking care of business on his property.

Michael has a long list of previous arrests, many of them containing violence. He is known to have a bad temper. The police came twice prior to dad's assault. The first time, Michael left and the police left. The second time, they arrived after Michael left the scene. The third time was after dad's assault. Apparently, Michael hit dad several times on the front landing of his apartment building. It was loud enough for the neighbors to hear. There was a brick wall close by and we assume he hit his head on that brick wall at some point in the assault.

Everyone in the neighborhood have only good things to say about my dad and love my dad. They are all very sorry for what happened.

Dad's medical status...

Dad's initial medical status was that he was unconscious with a very severe brain injury. According to Akron General brain surgeons, prognosis can be 100% recovery with time.

Here is a helpful story on brain injury and recovery: http://www.parade.com/health/2009/07/12-lee-woodruff-can-brains-be-saved.html

The criminal case
I have stayed in close communication with the detectives on his case and they have activated the fugitive task force, which means there are US marshals looking for Michael as well. There is a warrant for his arrest and witnesses to the crime. Crime stoppers also has a reward for information leading to his arrest.

Thank you for your prayers and support!

Has your family been through something tragic that changed your life? Your experience might be completely different from ours, but any tragedy can be life altering. I encourage you to reflect on an incident from your own life that you are still struggling to understand as you read through our story. You can ponder the answers, or even start a journal like I did, and hopefully God can use what He taught me during those dark days to help you as well.

> ➤ The first thing I encourage you to reflect on is the facts. What do you know to be true? Take some time and write them down, and then pray for God to help you understand what He is teaching you through these events.

July 23, 2009: Visiting Pity City

I am struggling today. One of my patients is a survivor of breast cancer and was sharing her story with me. She mentioned something helpful to me today. She said "I can visit 'pity city'…I just can't live there." I have to admit I felt like moving into "pity city" today! But, her words came at just the right time to remind me that it's okay to feel my feelings, but just not to let them control me. I have so much to learn…

July 23, 2009: Breakthrough to Hope

I felt like I had a breakthrough this morning. As I was journaling and praying, I felt God say to me that I need to focus on this being a transformational time for dad, emotionally and spiritually, and not to focus on what his physical and cognitive deficits will be as he recovers - that at the end of life, only one thing really matters…and that is our soul.

I have had peace and a sense from God from the beginning that Dad is okay. That his soul and spirit are okay and that Jesus is with him… that no matter what happens to him physically, Jesus is with him and is taking care of him. He is in good hands.

As I was praying this morning, God brought a scripture to my mind that I will now continue to hold on to for the duration of Dad's recovery. It is 2 Corinthians 4:16-18,

> *"Therefore we do not lose heart. Though outwardly we are wasting away, yet inwardly we are being renewed day by day. For our light and momentary troubles are achieving for us an eternal glory that far outweighs them all. So we fix our eyes not on what is seen, but on what is unseen. For what is seen is temporary, but what is unseen is eternal."*

What a paradigm shift!

Continue reading Finding Hope in the Midst of Tragedy and be encouraged as you read one family's journey to hope. Get your copy here:

http://www.amazon.com/dp/B008RSQFJC

Available in print and eBook versions.

Get Free Christian Books

Love getting FREE Christian books online? If so, sign up to get notified of new Christian book promotions and never miss out. Then, grab a cup of coffee and enjoy reading the free Christian books you download.

You will also get our FREE report, *"How to Find Free Christian Books Online"* that shows You 9 places you can get new books...for free!

Sign up at:
www.bodyandsoulpublishing.com/freebooks

Happy reading!

CJ and Shelley Hitz

C.J. and Shelley Hitz enjoy sharing God's Truth through their speaking engagements and their writing. On downtime, they enjoy spending time outdoors running, hiking and exploring God's beautiful creation.

To find out more about their ministry check out their website at www.BodyandSoulPublishing.com or to invite them to your next event go to www.ChristianSpeakers.tv.

Note from the Author: Reviews are gold to authors! If you have enjoyed this book, would you consider reviewing it on Amazon.com? Thank you!

Shelley's Contact Information

We would love to hear from you. Also, send your prayer requests, so that we can specifically pray for you!

Send us an e-mail or a letter to the following address:
shelley@shelleyhitz.com

Websites:

www.BodyandSoulPublishing.com
www.ShelleyHitz.com

Other Books by CJ and Shelley Hitz

Broken Crayons Still Color

A Life of Gratitude

21 Days of Gratitude Challenge

21 Days of Faith Challenge

21 Days of Generosity Challenge

Finding Hope in the Midst of Tragedy

Forgiveness Formula

Unshackled and Free

Mirror Mirror... Am I Beautiful?

Teen Devotionals... for Girls!

Fuel for the Soul

References

[1] Ten Boom, Corrie (with Jamie Buckingham) *Tramp for the Lord.* Christian Literature Crusade (Fort Washington, PA) and Fleming H Revell Company (Old Tappan, NJ), 1974, p. 9.

[2] Ibid

[3] Warren, Kay. Dangerous Surrender: What Happens When You Say Yes to God. Zondervan. 2007.

[4] Ten Boom, Corrie (with John and Elizabeth Sherrill). *The Hiding Place.* Chosen Books, 1971, p.6.

[5] Ebner, Gwen. *Wholeness for Spiritual Leaders. Physical, Spiritual and Emotional Self-Care.* CreateSpace, 2009, p.46.

[6] The Baylor Institute for Studies of Religion and Department of Sociology, Baylor University. *American Piety in the 21st Century:New Insights to the Depth and Complexity of Religion in the US.* Baylor University, September 2006, p.26-32. (http://www.baylor.edu/content/services/document.php/33304.pdf)

[7] Ibid.

[8] Ibid.

[9] Young, Wm. Paul. *The Shack. Where Tragedy Confronts Eternity.* Windblown Media, 2007, 126.

[10] Ebner, Gwen. *Wholeness for Spiritual Leaders. Physical, Spiritual and Emotional Self-Care.* CreateSpace, 2009, p.50.

[11] Mark Virkler offers an indepth study, *"How to Hear God's Voice"* that can be found at www.cwgministries.org.

[12] Bright, Bill. *God, Discover His Character.* New Life Publications, 1999, p.10